New Testament

POCKET GUIDE

CONTENTS

FEATURES

God speaks – The inspiration of the New
Testament   3
Matthew – A changed allegiance   6
Miracles of Jesus   10
John Mark – Deserter who returned   12
Scribes, Pharisees and Sadducees   15
Luke – Faithful companion   17
Israel's Roman rulers   19
Martha and Mary – Ministered to the
Master   21
Finding the parables   22
John – Beloved apostle   24
The "I am" statements of Jesus   26
Festival times in Israel   27
Stephen – Fearless and faithful   30
Romans – The Gospel explained   38
Paul – Apostle with unlimited horizons   42
Dating the New Testament   46
On active service   49
Aspects of prayer   50
The New Testament canon   53
Timothy – Making of a minister   54
James – Brother of the Lord   58
Jesus worshipped   61

INTRODUCTIONS and SUMMARIES

The four Gospels   4
Matthew's Gospel   7
Mark's Gospel   13
Luke's Gospel   18
John's Gospel   23
Acts   29
The Letters   35
Romans   37
1 Corinthians   40
2 Corinthians   43
Galatians   45
Ephesians   45
Philippians   48
Colossians   48
1 and 2 Thessalonians   49
1 and 2 Timothy   52

Titus   52
Philemon   53
Hebrews   55
James   57
1 and 2 Peter   57
1, 2 and 3 John   60
Jude   61
Revelation   63

OUTLINES

Matthew   5
Mark   11
Luke   16
John   23
Acts   28
Romans   36
1 Corinthians   39
2 Corinthians   39
Galatians   44
Ephesians   44
Philippians   47
Colossians   47
1 and 2 Thessalonians   47
1 and 2 Timothy   51
Titus   51
Philemon   51
Hebrews   54
James   56
1 and 2 Peter   56
1, 2 and 3 John   59
Jude   59
Revelation   62

MAPS

Events in Jesus' life   9
From trial to triumph   14
Peter's audience on the Day of Pentecost   31
Witnesses in Judea and Samaria   31
Paul's journeys   32
Letters to Churches   44
Timothy, pastor at Ephesus   51
The Churches Peter wrote to   56
The seven letters of Revelation   63

GOD SPEAKS — THE INSPIRATION OF THE NEW TESTAMENT

Looks, gestures, symbols – even music or art. All are means of expression. But it is through words that we can best and most precisely communicate what is on our heart and mind. God has chosen to speak to us in this way too.

In the Old Testament the prophets again and again spoke as God's messengers declaring: "This is the word of the Lord". Comments the writer to the Hebrews: "In the past God spoke to our forefathers through the prophets ... but in these last days he has spoken to us by his Son" (1:1). Jesus Himself saw His whole ministry in the light of the Scriptures which must be fulfilled (Luke 24:44). He plainly believed that what Scripture said, God said (eg. Matt. 19:5 and Gen. 2:24).

When the New Testament speaks of the Bible being inspired, this is what it means. A literal translation of 2 Timothy 3:16 is: "All Scripture is God-breathed". Each word in the original languages was given by God. In this God did not use His writers as typewriters at His "fingertips", but He took their personalities, skills and backgrounds, which He had shaped, and through them said exactly what He wanted to.

Paul may have had the Old Testament in mind when he wrote those famous words to Timothy, but the Church was certainly correct to see that they applied equally to God's written revelation of the New Covenant, the New Testament. The fact of apostolic authorship or association in most New Testament writings is a guarantee that they are God's words. They fulfil the promise of Jesus that the Holy Spirit would lead the Church into all truth (John 16:13). Paul wrote that the apostles' message was a revelation "by the Spirit to God's holy apostles and prophets" (Eph. 3:5 and see 1 Cor. 2:13) and for Peter there was no distinction between Paul's letters and the other (Old Testament) Scriptures (2 Peter 3:16).

The New Testament closes with the Book of Revelation which affirms its divine origin in the first verse: it is "the revelation of Jesus Christ which God gave".

THE FOUR GOSPELS

Almost all we know of Jesus' earthly life is to be found here. As the eye-witnesses of Jesus were passing from the scene, the Gospels were written as a permanent witness to Jesus' life and teaching. They are not a biography. They do not tell us all we might be curious about. There is, for example, only one event recorded from the years between Jesus' infancy and public ministry when He was about 30. The reason for this lies in the authors' intentions. They were writing a Gospel (Greek – *euangelion*) or "Good News" of Jesus. Their aim – to point others to the Son of God and Saviour in whom they had trusted. They put to paper, therefore, what their readers needed to know to believe and have life in Him.

The New Testament has four Gospel accounts. Three – Matthew, Mark and Luke, have a great deal of common material. They are often referred to as the "synoptic" Gospels because they follow a similar pattern. John's Gospel, however, has much unique content. It revolves especially around events in Jerusalem at festival times and goes deepest into Jesus' teaching about Himself. Each Gospel writer has his own emphasis and helps to give a fuller picture of the Lord. In fact, the early Church would have spoken of only one Gospel (Col. 1:23; Gal. 1:6–7) – one Gospel; four accounts – all four bearing witness to the one Good News about Jesus.

MATTHEW

The birth and childhood of Jesus Christ

Genealogy of Christ — 1:1–17
Birth of Christ — 1:18–25
Visit of the Magi — 2:1–12
Escape to Egypt and massacre of the infants — 2:13–18
Return to Nazareth — 2:19–23

The beginning of Jesus' ministry

John the Baptist prepares the way — 3:1–12
Baptism of Christ — 3:13–17
Temptation of Christ — 4:1–11

The ministry of Jesus

A – In Galilee:

Jesus begins to preach — 4:12–17
Call of four disciples — 4:18–22
General summary of the Galilean ministry — 4:23–25
Sermon on the Mount — 5:1—7:29
Miracles and related teaching — 8:1—9:38
Jesus sends out the 12 — 10:1–42
Jesus and John the Baptist — 11:1–19
Rebuke to the unrepentant — 11:20–24
Rest for the weary — 11:25–30
Opposition from the Pharisees — 12:1–50
Parables on the Kingdom — 13:1–52
A prophet without honour — 13:53–58
John the Baptist beheaded — 14:1–12
Feeding the 5,000 — 14:13–21
Jesus walks on the water — 14:22–36
Conflict with the Pharisees over tradition — 15:1–20
Faith of the Canaanite woman — 15:21–28
Feeding the 4,000 — 15:29–39
Conflict with the Pharisees and Sadducees — 16:1–12
Peter's confession of Christ — 16:13–20
Jesus predicts His death — 16:21–28
The transfiguration — 17:1–13
Instruction of the 12 — 17:14—18:35

B – In Perea:

Teaching on divorce — 19:1–12
Blessing the little children — 19:13–15
The rich young man — 19:16–30
Parable of the workers in the vineyard — 20:1–16

C – In Judea:

Jesus speaks of His death and on servanthood — 20:17–28
Two blind men healed — 20:29–34

Jesus' ministry in Jerusalem

Triumphal entry — 21:1–11
Cleansing of the Temple — 21:12–17
A barren fig-tree cursed — 21:18–22
Jesus' authority questioned — 21:23–27
Parables of judgment — 21:28—22:14
Questioned by Pharisees and Sadducees — 22:15–46
Jesus denounces the Pharisees — 23:1–39
Teaching about the end of the age — 24:1—25:46

The last days of Jesus

Plot against Jesus — 26:1–16
The Last Supper — 26:17–30
Jesus predicts Peter's denial — 26:31–35
Events in Gethsemane — 26:36–56
Before the Sanhedrin — 26:57–68
Peter's denial — 26:69–75
Judas hangs himself — 27:1–10
Jesus before Pilate — 27:11–26
The crucifixion — 27:27–56
Burial — 27:57–66

The resurrection of Jesus

The resurrection — 28:1–10
The guards' report — 28:11–15
The Great Commission — 28:16–20

Matthew —
A changed allegiance

Matthew, also called Levi (Mark 2:14, Luke 5:27) was the tax-collector whom Jesus called to be a disciple. Levi probably changed his name to Matthew ("gift of Yahweh") when this happened. Jesus' choice of a Jewish tax-collector in the service of the Romans is remarkable for they were much hated by their own countrymen. However, his skill at writing and record-keeping would be of great value.

Apart from mentions of Matthew in the lists of the apostles, we hear no more of him after he held a banquet for Jesus, attended by many tax-collectors, at his house (Luke 5:29–32).

Matthew's Gospel

This was the most highly valued Gospel in the Early Church. New believers needed instruction and Matthew's Gospel, with its emphasis on Christ's teaching, provided it. This Gospel also had apostolic authority: from earliest times it was credited to Matthew, the apostle and former tax-collector.

Writing for a Jewish readership, Matthew centres on Jesus as the Christ, the kingly Messiah promised by Old Testament prophecy. Mistaken expectations of a political liberator from foreign rule are corrected as Matthew presents Jesus' teaching on the true nature and principles of the kingdom of heaven.

Faith in Jesus, Matthew showed, involved no rejection of the Old Testament by Jewish believers – it was the very fulfilment of it and the goal to which it pointed.

The Messiah's mission

Matthew establishes Jesus by His genealogy as the heir to the throne of David. The conception of Jesus by the Holy Spirit is explained and Magi come to attend "the King of the Jews".

The baptism by John and the temptation in the desert lead into Jesus' public ministry and the first section of teaching – the Sermon on the Mount. Miracles of healing and the calming of the storm on Galilee interrupt the teaching before we see Jesus preparing the Twelve for evangelism. Unbelief and rejection will be common, Jesus warns, and subsequent incidents show the Lord Himself experiencing this.

After addressing thousands in Galilee, Jesus withdraws with His disciples to Caesarea Philippi and speaks more of His mission and the nature of the kingdom. In Jerusalem "the Son of Man" will be condemned to death, crucified and rise to life on the third day. During this time of disclosure Jesus takes three disciples up a mountain and is transfigured before them.

Another teaching section follows before Jesus begins His last journey to Jerusalem. This leads us to the climax of His ministry.

At the entry into Jerusalem the crowds clearly proclaim their hopes of Jesus as the Messiah. The religious officials are immediately on the attack, questioning Jesus' authority. The Lord replies with a series of parables before He takes His disciples to the Mount of Olives to give them special teaching on the Second Coming.

The plot against Him gathers pace and opportunity through the betrayal by Judas. An unwilling Pilate hands Jesus over to be crucified, but on the first day of the week the women meet with the risen Christ.

The closing words are those of the King who has all authority in heaven and on earth, commissioning His disciples to extend His kingdom to all nations.

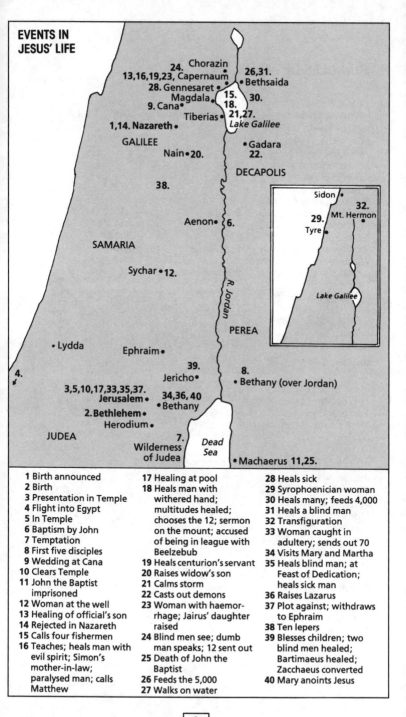

EVENTS IN JESUS' LIFE

24. Chorazin
13,16,19,23. Capernaum **26,31.**
28. Gennesaret • Bethsaida
Magdala **15. 30.**
9. Cana **18.**
Tiberias **21,27.**
Lake Galilee
1,14. Nazareth •

GALILEE

Nain • **20.**
• Gadara
22.

DECAPOLIS

38.

Sidon • **32.**
29. Mt. Hermon
Aenon • **6.** Tyre •

SAMARIA

Sychar • **12.** *Lake Galilee*

R. Jordan

PEREA

• Lydda
Ephraim •
39. **8.**
Jericho • • Bethany (over Jordan)
3,5,10,17,33,35,37.
Jerusalem • **34,36,40**
2. Bethlehem • • Bethany
Herodium •
7.
JUDEA Wilderness *Dead*
of Judea *Sea* • Machaerus **11,25.**

1 Birth announced	17 Healing at pool	28 Heals sick
2 Birth	18 Heals man with	29 Syrophoenician woman
3 Presentation in Temple	withered hand;	30 Heals many; feeds 4,000
4 Flight into Egypt	multitudes healed;	31 Heals a blind man
5 In Temple	chooses the 12; sermon	32 Transfiguration
6 Baptism by John	on the mount; accused	33 Woman caught in
7 Temptation	of being in league with	adultery; sends out 70
8 First five disciples	Beelzebub	34 Visits Mary and Martha
9 Wedding at Cana	19 Heals centurion's servant	35 Heals blind man; at
10 Clears Temple	20 Raises widow's son	Feast of Dedication;
11 John the Baptist	21 Calms storm	heals sick man
imprisoned	22 Casts out demons	36 Raises Lazarus
12 Woman at the well	23 Woman with haemor-	37 Plot against; withdraws
13 Healing of official's son	rhage; Jairus' daughter	to Ephraim
14 Rejected in Nazareth	raised	38 Ten lepers
15 Calls four fishermen	24 Blind men see; dumb	39 Blesses children; two
16 Teaches; heals man with	man speaks; 12 sent out	blind men healed;
evil spirit; Simon's	25 Death of John the	Bartimaeus healed;
mother-in-law;	Baptist	Zacchaeus converted
paralysed man; calls	26 Feeds the 5,000	40 Mary anoints Jesus
Matthew	27 Walks on water	

MIRACLES OF JESUS

Individuals healed	Matthew	Mark	Luke	John
Official's son				4:46—54
Man with an evil spirit		1:23—27	4:33—36	
Peter's mother-in-law	8:14—15	1:30—31	4:38—39	
Man with leprosy	8:2—4	1:40—45	5:12—14	
Paralysed man	9:1—8	2:1—12	5:17—26	
Invalid at the pool				5:1—15
Man with shrivelled hand	12:9—14			
Centurion's servant	8:5—13		7:1—10	
Raising widow's son			7:11—17	
Blind and mute demoniac	12:22		11:14	
Raising Jairus' daughter	9:18—26	5:21—43	8:40—56	
Woman with haemorrhage	9:20—22	5:25—34	8:43—48	
A mute demoniac	9:32—34			
Canaanite or Syrophoenician woman's daughter	15:21—28	7:24—30		
Deaf and mute man		7:31—37		
A blind man		8:22—26		
A boy with a demon	17:14—18	9:17—29	9:37—43	

Groups healed	Matthew	Mark	Luke	John
Many in Capernaum	8:16—17	1:32—34	4:40—41	
Many by Sea of Galilee		3:7—12		
Two demon-possessed men	8:28—34	5:1—20	8:26—39	
Two blind men	9:27—31			
Many on mountainside by Galilee	15:29—31			
Ten lepers			17:11—19	
Two blind men	20:29—34	10:46—52		

Jesus healing the blind man. 13th C. Italian.

Power over nature	Matthew	Mark	Luke	John
Water changed to wine				2:1—11
Catch of fish			5:1—7	
Storm stilled	8:23—27	4:35—41	8:22—25	
Feeding 5,000	14:15—21	6:35—44	9:12—17	6:5—13
Walking on Sea of Galilee	14:25—33	6:47—52		6:16—22
Feeding 4,000	15:32—38	8:1—10		
Coin in the fish's mouth	17:24—27			
Cursing the fig-tree	21:18—22			
Second catch of fish				21:4—6

	Matthew	Mark	Luke	John
The resurrection of Jesus	28:1—10	16:1—9	24:1—43	20:1—30
Jesus ascends to the Father		16:19	24:50—51	

MARK

The preparation for Jesus' ministry
John the Baptist	1:1–8
Jesus' baptism and temptation	1:9–13

Christ's ministry in Galilee
The first disciples	1:14–20
First Galilean tour	1:21–45
A paralytic healed	2:1–12
Calling of Levi	2:13–17
Questions on fasting	2:18—3:6
The 12 appointed	3:7–19
Teachers of the law	3:20–30
Jesus' family	3:31–35
Parables by the lake	4:1–34
Calming the storm	4:35–41
Healing a demon-possessed man	5:1–20
Jairus' daughter	5:21–43
Jesus commissions the 12	6:1–13
John the Baptist beheaded	6:14–29

Jesus' withdrawals from Galilee
Feeding the 5,000	6:30–44
Walking on the water	6:45–56
What makes a man unclean	7:1–23
Withdrawal to Tyre	7:24–30
4,000 fed	7:31—8:21
Healing a blind man	8:22–26
Jesus predicts His death	8:27—9:1

The transfiguration	9:2–13
Healing a boy with an evil spirit	9:14–29
Lessons for the 12	9:30–50

Christ's ministry in Perea
Teaching on divorce	10:1–12
Jesus welcomes little children	10:13–16
The rich young man	10:17–31
The Son of Man's mission	10:32–45
Blind Bartimaeus healed	10:46–52

Ministry in Jerusalem
Triumphal entry	11:1–11
Cleansing the Temple; the fig-tree	11:12–26
Controversies with the religious leaders	11:27—12:44
The end of the age	13:1–37

Christ's death and resurrection
Treachery and devotion	14:1–11
The Lord's Supper	14:12–26
Gethsemane and Jesus' arrest	14:27–52
The trials and crucifixion	14:53—15:41
The burial	15:42–47
The resurrection	16:1–20

John Mark —
Deserter who returned

"John" was his Jewish name, "Mark" his Roman.
He came from Jerusalem where the early church
would meet at his mother's house (Acts 12:12). He
accompanied Paul and Barnabas (his cousin) on
their first missionary journey but returned home
during it. Paul would not take him on his second
trip but Barnabas gave him another chance, taking
Mark with him to visit the believers in Cyprus.
Relations with Paul were later restored and Mark's
work in the Gospel recognised. In prison Paul
found him a great comfort and came to see him as
a valued co-labourer (Col. 4:10, 11; 2 Tim. 4:11).
Peter, whose companion he became, loved him as
his own son (1 Peter 5:13).

Mark's Gospel

Mark's Gospel is the Gospel of action. His fast-moving account concentrates primarily on Jesus' deeds. Only one long teaching message is recorded and four parables compared to Matthew's 18 and Luke's 19. A special vividness characterises the description of events with details such as the looks and gestures of Jesus. There is a note of urgency too – the Greek word *euthys* ("immediately", "at once", "as soon as" in NIV) appears a striking 40 times.

None of this is surprising when we consider the probable circumstances under which this Gospel was written. Strong early tradition says that the Gospel was Mark's transmission of the teaching of Peter. This suits the "eye-witness" style reporting. The Gospel is thought to have been written in Rome shortly before the destruction of Jerusalem in AD 70, if not earlier.

Mark seems to have had Roman Christians in mind as his readers – he explains many Jewish terms and customs, but he assumes their belief that Jesus is the Son of God at the outset.

To these readers Mark presents Jesus as the mighty conqueror and Suffering Servant of the Lord.

The Son who serves

Mark's Gospel begins with the "road-building" of John the Baptist. After brief synopses of the baptism and temptation, Mark embarks on Jesus' Galilean ministry of proclaiming the good news in word and deed. Crowds flock to hear Him, but Jesus warns that the cost of discipleship is self-denial and whole-hearted commitment to Him (8:34).

The Twelve were slow to appreciate what this entailed, and still hankered after honours for themselves (9:34; 10:37). Jesus' reply to James and John's question about the way to the top must have brought them up with a jolt. The way of honour is the way of service, He said, for the Son of Man came to give His life as a ransom for many.

In Jerusalem the Lord talks again of His death, but to the Pharisees. To them He speaks in the parable of the tenants who murdered the son of the vineyard owner – its message is not lost on them.

After the Lord's Mount of Olives teaching on His Second Coming, Mark moves to the final scenes of His life on earth and the fulfilment of Jesus' predictions of His death and resurrection.

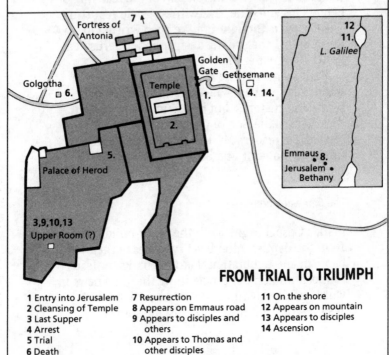

FROM TRIAL TO TRIUMPH

1 Entry into Jerusalem
2 Cleansing of Temple
3 Last Supper
4 Arrest
5 Trial
6 Death
7 Resurrection
8 Appears on Emmaus road
9 Appears to disciples and others
10 Appears to Thomas and other disciples
11 On the shore
12 Appears on mountain
13 Appears to disciples
14 Ascension

SCRIBES, PHARISEES AND SADDUCEES

The Scribes, also called lawyers or teachers (Rabbis), originated in pre-exilic times (before 720 BC) as government officials. From the time of Ezra (fifth century BC), however, increasingly they were copiers and interpreters of the Law of Moses. They decided how it should be applied to everyday life and supplemented it so that it was impossible to break unknowingly. Thinking they had rightly interpreted the Law, they and their followers, the Pharisees, gave their rules equal authority with Scripture. Jesus, however, accused them of nullifying God's Word by their traditions (Mark 7:5–23). Most opposed Christ (Matt. 21:15) – though not all (Matt. 8:19).

The Pharisees ("separated ones") had emerged in the second century before Christ. They had banded together with the aim of preserving the purity of the faith and keeping most strictly to the duties of the Law as laid down by the Scribes. In the time of the Herods there were about 6,000 drawn mostly from the lower middle and better artisan classes. Often proud of their own righteousness, many despised those who did not keep their burdensome laws. They constantly clashed with Jesus because He did not follow their strict code (eg. Matt. 9:11; 12:2). They received from Jesus some of His most scathing criticism (Matt. 23:27–28). There were godly Pharisees, though: Nicodemus was a Pharisee, as was Paul.

The Sadducees were a smaller and more elite group socially. Nearly all were priests, some holding office in the Sanhedrin. The New Testament mentions them by name only about a dozen times, but in its references to the chief priests practically the same people are meant. They were on good terms with their Roman rulers and more concerned with political stability than religious observance. The rationalists of their day – they denied the resurrection of the body, immortality and judgment. Their views could cause heated arguments with the Pharisees, a fact Paul made use of when arrested in Jerusalem (Acts 23:6–7). Yet they joined the Pharisees in their plot to murder Jesus and were fierce in their persecution of the early Church.

LUKE

Introduction	1:1–4

The announcement of the Saviour

John the Baptist's birth foretold	1:5–25
Jesus' birth foretold	1:26–56
The birth of John the Baptist	1:57–80
The birth of Jesus	2:1–20
Presentation in the Temple	2:21–40
The boy Jesus at the Temple	2:41–52

The appearance of the Saviour

John prepares the way	3:1–20
Baptism and genealogy of Jesus	3:21–38
The temptation	4:1–13

Jesus' public ministry

Rejection in Nazareth	4:14–30
Teaching and healing	4:31–44
The first disciples	5:1–11
Power to forgive sins	5:12–32
Fasting and the Sabbath	5:33—6:11
Choosing the 12	6:12–19
The way of discipleship	6:20–49
The centurion's servant; the widow's son	7:1–17
John the Baptist's question	7:18–35
Jesus anointed by a sinful woman	7:36–50
Our response to the Word	8:1–21
Stilling the storm	8:22–25
Miracles of healing	8:26–56

Jesus' ministry in Galilee

Jesus sends out the 12	9:1–9
Feeding the 5,000	9:10–17
Peter's confession; the transfiguration	9:18–36
A boy with an evil spirit healed	9:37–45

The journey to Jerusalem

The cost of discipleship	9:46–62
Jesus sends the 72	10:1–16
The privileges of discipleship	10:17–24
The good Samaritan	10:25–37
Martha and Mary	10:38–42
Prayer to the Father	11:1–13
Unbelief condemned	11:14–54

Warnings and encouragements	12:1–34
Readiness for the Master's return	12:35—13:9
A crippled woman healed	13:10–17
The narrow door	13:18–30
Jesus' sorrow for Jerusalem	13:31–35
The parable of the banquet	14:1–24
True commitment	14:25–35
The lost sheep; the lost coin; the lost son	15:1–32
Parable of the shrewd manager	16:1–13

The journey to Jerusalem

Warnings to the rich	16:14–31
The way of service	17:1–10
Ten lepers healed	17:11–19
The Second Coming	17:20–37
Persistence and humility	18:1–14
Entry into God's Kingdom	18:15–30
Jesus predicts His death	18:31–34
Jericho: a blind beggar and Zacchaeus	18:35—19:10
The parable of the ten minas	19:11–27

Arrival in Jerusalem

The triumphal entry	19:28–44
Jesus answers His enemies' challenges	19:45—20:47
Signs of the end of the age	21:1–37

The crucifixion

Jesus' betrayer	22:1–6
The Last Supper	22:7–38
Jesus prays on the Mount of Olives	22:39–46
Jesus arrested	22:47–53
Peter's denial	22:54–62
Jesus before Pilate and Herod	22:63—23:25
The crucifixion	23:26–49
Jesus' burial	23:50–56

The resurrection

The empty tomb	24:1–12
The road to Emmaus	24:13–35
Jesus appears to the disciples	24:36–49
The ascension	24:50–53

Luke –
Faithful companion

Paul described him as "our dear friend Luke, the doctor" (Col. 4:14). Luke travelled alongside Paul on two stages of his missionary journeys and stayed with him as he headed for sure arrest in Jerusalem. He continued with him through his imprisonment in Caesarea and to the end in Rome. It was probably Paul's detention at Caesarea (about AD 60) that provided Luke with the opportunity to write his Gospel.

Luke's Gospel

Luke presents a Gospel for all nations. Acts is the sequel, the second part of his history of Christian beginnings.

The two books name their audience, Theophilus, though not their author. In common with the other Gospels, the writer is not named in the Scriptures themselves, but there is little doubt that Luke, the doctor and Paul's companion, was responsible. The Gospel was penned by an educated and literate hand: a writer, too, with a special interest in disease and healing. His Gospel suggests his warmth of heart. Luke focuses on the kindness of Jesus towards the weak, the suffering and the outcast.

Luke writes to Roman official Theophilus to provide a thoroughly reliable historical document from the testimony of eye-witnesses to the events. In so doing, he has given us the fullest life story of Jesus and much teaching that is unique to this Gospel.

Good news to the poor

Luke's account of Jesus' birth is fuller than Matthew's and written from Mary's perspective. It is also the only Gospel which tells us anything of Jesus' boyhood. The source of much of Luke's information must have been Mary herself.

In the preaching of John the Baptist Luke alone records John's application of repentance to every-day living (3:10–14). True repentance is shown in generosity, honesty, fairness and contentment.

Jesus' family line is traced back to Adam to identify Him as the Saviour, not for the seed of

ISRAEL'S ROMAN RULERS

Herod the Great

HEROD THE GREAT

The son of an Idumean father and a Nabatean (Arab) mother, Herod had taken control of Judea by 37 BC. The order he maintained in the face of Jewish hatred of Rome shows his remarkable ability, but it was combined with unrestrained ruthlessness. He ordered the death of his favourite wife and three of his sons when they were seen as threats to himself. His murder of the infants (Matthew 2:16) fits the picture given by Jewish historian Josephus of a king driven in his last years by delusions of persecution and uncontrollable outbursts of violence. After his death in 4 BC, his kingdom was divided between his three sons.

ARCHELAUS

Archelaus became ruler of Judea and Idumea. He inherited his father's weaknesses without his skill. Bloody attempts to crush Jewish discontent led to an uprising. Jesus' family returning from Egypt went directly to Nazareth to avoid Archelaus (Matthew 2:22). Archelaus was banished for incompetency in AD 6. Roman officers called procurators replaced him. These included **Pontius Pilate** (AD 26–36), **Felix** (AD 52–60) and **Festus** (AD 60–62).

Pontius Pilate

HEROD ANTIPAS

Galilee and Perea were given to Antipas. Like his father, he was a political wheeler-dealer. Jesus called him "that fox" (Luke 13:22). He took Herodias, his half-brother's wife, as his queen. John the Baptist's denunciation of this led to John's death (Mark 6). This is the Herod to whom Jesus was sent by Pilate (Luke 23:8). He retained his power until AD 39.

PHILIP

Governor of the out-of-the-way districts of Iturea and Trachonitis, Philip seems to have been a humane and just ruler. He died in AD 34.

Philip

HEROD AGRIPPA I

A grandson of Herod I, Agrippa was granted Philip's province in AD 39 and later Galilee and Perea. After his agonising death in AD 46 (Acts 12:20–23), Palestine came wholly under Roman rule.

Under the rule of Roman governors, Jewish nationalism gathered momentum in Judea, leading to a general rebellion in AD 66. This was crushed with the near-complete destruction of Jerusalem in AD 70.

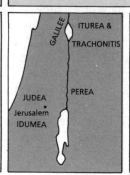

GALILEE — ITUREA & TRACHONITIS — PEREA — JUDEA — Jerusalem — IDUMEA

HEROD AGRIPPA II

Son of Agrippa I, he became ruler of territory in the north-east of Palestine. He appears in Acts 25 as Festus' guest to hear Paul's defence.

Abraham alone, but for all mankind. At Nazareth Jesus announces the fulfilment of the promised "year of the Lord's favour" in Himself. The incidents of healing, deliverance and forgiveness of sin demonstrate that this time has truly come.

Women are prominent in the third Gospel. Luke alone tells us at this point of the women who accompanied the Lord with the Twelve and who helped to support them from their own means.

After Jesus commissions the Twelve and sends the 72 ahead towards Jerusalem, Luke presents nearly eight chapters devoted to Jesus' preaching. Much was given in parables and many are uniquely recorded in this Gospel.

Luke gives special prominence to prayer in his account. The story of the man who calls at midnight, the thankfulness of the Samaritan healed of leprosy and Luke's description of the transfiguration show his devotional emphasis.

The conversion of Zacchaeus in Jericho is another detail of the Lord's ministry only noted in this Gospel. From Jericho the Lord comes to Jerusalem where His preaching becomes a magnet to the hostile religious leaders. He is betrayed, arrested and condemned by a crowd insistent on His execution.

It is Luke who tells us of the criminal crucified at Jesus' side who asked for salvation. Jesus' assuring words of reply have given hope to thousands since.

At Jesus' death darkness comes over the land. Later He is buried in Joseph of Arimathea's borrowed sepulchre, before the cataclysmic event that is to occur on the third day.

Three amazing incidents – the women's encounter with the angels at the empty tomb, the meeting with Jesus on the Emmaus road and the appearance of the Lord to Simon – bring home to the disciples the glorious news that Jesus is risen! Then He appears to them, standing in their midst, so that the joy and wonder of His resurrection can come to them all.

The details of the next weeks are compressed into a few verses which Luke expands on in The Acts of the Apostles. During these 40 days Jesus opens the disciples' minds to the Scriptures, shows how He has fulfilled them and explains the message of repentance and forgiveness they are to preach when the Holy Spirit is poured out. From Bethany the Lord ascends before their eyes and is taken up into heaven.

Martha and Mary — Ministered to the Master

Martha, Mary and Lazarus kept open house at their Bethany home outside Jerusalem.

When visiting Jerusalem, as He often did, the Lord must have greatly valued the hospitality which was always available to Him there. It was a perfect retreat from the hustle and bustle of the city and from the mounting opposition of the religious leaders.

Although sisters, Mary and Martha were opposites in temperament. Martha, probably the elder of the two, appears to have been energetic and practical, while Mary was more contemplative. Mary delighted to sit at the Lord's feet and drink in His teaching. As her spiritual life deepened in His presence, she became one of His most devoted followers.

The apostle John describes the relationship of Jesus with this family very simply: "Jesus loved Martha and her sister and Lazarus" (John 11:5).

PARABLES

Jesus and farmer
10th C. German

Finding the Parables

	Matthew	Mark	Luke
The two debtors			7:41–43
The sower	13:3–8	4:4–8	8:5–8
The weeds	13:24–30		
The growing seed		4:26–29	
The barren fig tree			13:6–9
The mustard seed	13:31–32	4:3–32	13:18–19
The yeast	13:33		13:20–21
The hidden treasure	13:44		
The pearl	13:45–46		
The drag net	13:47–50		
The good Samaritan			10:30–37
The friend at midnight			11:5–8
The rich fool			12:16–21
The lowest seat at the feast			14:7–11
The great banquet			14:15–24
The lost sheep	18:12–14		15:3–7
The unmerciful servant	18:23–25		
The lost coin			15:8–10
The lost son			15:11–32
The shrewd manager			16:1–9
The rich man and Lazarus			16:19–31
Unprofitable servants			17:7–10
The unjust judge			18:1–8
The Pharisee and the tax collector			18:9–14
The workers in the vineyard	20:1–16		
The ten minas			19:11–27
The two sons	21:28–32		
The wicked tenants	21:33–34	12:1–12	20:9–18
The watchful porter		13:34–37	
The wedding banquet	22:1–14		
The faithful servant	24:45–51		12:42–48
The ten virgins	25:1–13		
The talents	25:14–30		

The word comes from the Greek verb *parabállo*, composed of
the preposition *para* (beside) and the verb *bállo* (to cast). A
parable is thus a comparison of two objects for the purpose of
teaching.

Only Jesus Himself used parables in the New Testament.
When He was asked by His disciples why He spoke in this way,
He explained their purpose: parables reveal truth to the
spiritual and ready mind and at the same time conceal it from
others (Matt. 13:11; Luke 8:10).

JOHN

**Prologue: the Word
became flesh**   1:1–18

Christ's ministry in the world
John the Baptist's
testimony   1:19–36
The gathering of disciples   1:37–51
The wedding at Cana   2:1–11
Clearing the Temple   2:12–25
Nicodemus' question   3:1–21
Further testimony from
John the Baptist   3:22–36
The Samaritan woman   4:1–42
Jesus heals an official's son 4:43–54
The healing at the pool   5:1–15
Life through the Son   5:16–47
Feeding the 5,000   6:1–15
Jesus walks on the water   6:16–24
The bread of life   6:25–59
Many desert Jesus   6:60–71
Jesus teaches at the Feast
of Tabernacles   7:1–27

Christ's ministry in the world
Unbelief of the Jewish
leaders   7:28–53
The woman taken in
adultery   8:1–11
The validity of Jesus'
testimony   8:12–30
Children of Abraham and
children of the devil   8:31–47
Jesus' claims about Himself   8:48–59
A blind man sees   9:1–41
The Shepherd and His flock   10:1–21
Rejection by the Jewish
leaders   10:22–42

The raising of Lazarus   11:1–44
The plot to kill Jesus   11:45–57
Jesus anointed at Bethany   12:1–11
The triumphal entry   12:12–19
Jesus predicts His death   12:20–50

Christ's ministry to His own
Jesus washes His disciples'
feet   13:1–17
Jesus predicts His betrayal   13:18–30
The upper room discourse   13:31—14:31
Jesus the true vine   15:1–17
Warning of opposition   15:18—16:4
The promise of the Holy
Spirit   16:5–15
Grief will turn to joy   16:16–33
Jesus prays for His
disciples   17:1–26

Trial, death and resurrection
Betrayal and arrest   18:1–14
Jesus is questioned and
Peter's denial   18:15–27
Jesus before Pilate   18:28–40
Jesus is handed over to the
Jews   19:1–16
The crucifixion   19:17–37
The burial   19:38–42
The empty tomb   20:1–9
Jesus appears to Mary   20:10–18
Jesus appears to His
disciples   20:19–31
Jesus appears by the Sea of
Galilee   21:1–14
Peter is reinstated   21:15–25

John –
Beloved apostle

When Jesus started to gather His disciples, He
called two pairs of brothers – Simon and Andrew
and James and John. John was the son of Zebedee
and Salome and the younger brother of James.
Both of these Galilean fishermen seem to have
been volatile characters: their anger at the
Samaritans who refused Jesus hospitality (Luke
9:54) suggests that the Lord had given them the
name "Boanerges" – sons of thunder (Mark 3:17) –
with good reason.

Together with James and Peter, John was
especially privileged within the 12. They were
chosen to be present when Jesus raised Jairus'
daughter from the dead, at the transfiguration, and
at Gethsemane. To John Jesus committed the care
of Mary, His mother, as He hung upon the cross
(John 19:26–27). John knew Jesus as few others did
and, in his Gospel, he shares that knowledge with
us.

John's Gospel

From the first striking words of John 1:1 we see John's emphasis on the person of Jesus as God in human form. Far more than the other Gospel authors he seeks to interpret and bring out the meaning of events to the end that readers will believe in the Christ and have eternal life in His name (John 20:30–31).

John draws our attention primarily to Jesus' sayings about Himself. John includes Jesus' 11 "I am" statements but none of His parables. Another difference from the other Gospels is John's concentration on the Lord's ministry in and around Jerusalem, rather than on events in Galilee.

The Gospel author describes himself as "the disciple whom Jesus loved" (John 21:20, 24). He was one of the Twelve and one of the closest to Jesus. Strong evidence within the Gospel points to the apostle John as the writer as the second century Church Fathers also asserted. They tell us John wrote or dictated his account in Ephesus in present-day Turkey. If they were right, the Gospel's first readers would have been mostly Gentiles. This would help us understand John's explanations of Jewish customs.

That you may believe

John's prologue proclaims the miracle of the incarnation – through the Son of God we have fellowship with the Father and have received blessing upon blessing. From his own testimony the author passes to John the Baptist's declaration – "Look, the Lamb of God, who takes away the sin of the world!"

THE "I AM" STATEMENTS OF JESUS

John 6:35	The Bread of Life
8:12	Light of the World
8:58	Before Abraham was
10:7	The Door
10:11	The Good Shepherd
10:36	The Son of God
11:25	The Resurrection and the Life
14:6	The Way, the truth and the Life
15:1	The Vine

John records two famous conversations with individuals – Nicodemus and the woman of Samaria. In the two interviews – with a respectable Jew and an outcast foreigner – the Holy Spirit shows us the breadth of the offer of salvation given regardless of status, class or race.

Jesus' testimony to Himself is much more direct in John's Gospel than in the synoptic accounts. It seems that the Lord's teaching style varied at different points in His ministry. Here, without using parables to convey the truth, Jesus' claims to be the Son of God, the Saviour and judge of men, are straight and clear (5:24).

Moving on from the public ministry, John concentrates chapters 13–16 on Jesus' last words to the Twelve. They begin with a demonstration. Jesus, the Master, washes the feet of His disciples. Then He speaks of His betrayal. He must return to the Father, He says, but He will send the Holy Spirit to live within them. He will remind them of all Jesus has said and lead them into all truth. In the Old Testament Israel was pictured as the vine that so often failed to bear fruit. Jesus tells His disciples that He is the true vine and they the branches. They will produce a rich crop as they remain in Him. The world will not love them for this. It has hated Jesus, the Master, and will hate the servants too.

In Jesus' high priestly prayer (ch. 17) the Lord prays for His disciples – not just His disciples then, but all who will come to trust in Him through the centuries (v. 20).

Jesus is then arrested. Tried by the Sanhedrin and by Pilate, the Lord shows us that it is really He who is in control of the situation – their power is only given at the Father's permission (15:11).

John describes the death Jesus died for us and the resurrection appearances that gave certainty to even the sceptical Thomas. His confession of faith and submission to Christ is an example of John's purpose in writing "... that you may believe that Jesus is the Christ, the Son of God, and that by believing you may have life in His name".

FESTIVAL TIMES IN ISRAEL

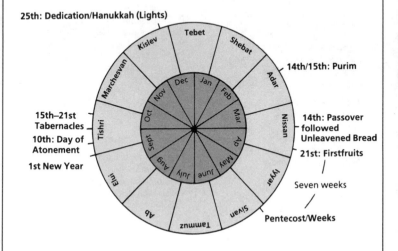

25th: Dedication/Hanukkah (Lights)

14th/15th: Purim

14th: Passover followed Unleavened Bread

21st: Firstfruits

Seven weeks

Pentecost/Weeks

15th–21st Tabernacles
10th: Day of Atonement
1st New Year

ACTS

The birth of the church in Jerusalem
From resurrection to
ascension   1:1–11
Matthias replaces Judas   1:12–26
The Holy Spirit comes at
Pentecost   2:1–13
Peter addresses the crowd   2:14–41
The life of the believers   2:42–47
Peter heals the crippled
beggar   3:1–10
Peter bears witness to Jesus 3:11–26
Before the Sanhedrin   4:1–22
The believers pray and
share together   4:23–37
Ananias and Sapphira   5:1–11
Signs, wonders and
persecutions   5:12–33
Gamaliel's counsel   5:34–42
Seven assistants appointed 6:1–7
Stephen arouses
opposition   6:8–15
Stephen's speech and
martyrdom   7:1–60

The Gospel spreads
Saul's persecution   8:1–3
Philip's ministry in Samaria 8:4–8
Simon the sorcerer   8:9–25
The Ethiopian treasurer   8:26–40
Saul's conversion   9:1–19
Saul bears witness in
Damascus and Jerusalem   9:20–31
Peter's ministry in Lydda
and Joppa   9:32–43

The Gospel for all men
Peter and the Gentile
centurion   10:1–48
The apostles approve
Peter's action   11:1–18
Antioch – the first Gentile
church   11:19–30
Peter's imprisonment and
escape   12:1–19
Death of Herod   12:20–25

The first missionary journey
Barnabas and Saul on
Cyprus   13:1–12
Paul in Pisidian Antioch   13:13–44
The jealousy of the Jews is
aroused   13:45–52
Mixed reception at Iconium 14:1–7
In Lystra and Derbe   14:8–20
Return to Syrian Antioch   14:21–28
The Council in Jerusalem   15:1–35

The second missionary journey
Paul and Barnabas disagree 15:36–41
Timothy joins Paul and Silas 16:1–5
Paul's vision   16:6–10

Paul takes the Gospel to Europe
Great events in Philippi   16:11–40
In Thessalonica and Berea 17:1–15
Paul proclaims to the
Athenians their "unknown
God"   17:16–34
Corinth   18:1–17
Priscilla, Aquila and Apollos 18:18–28
Events in Ephesus   19:1–41
Paul sets out for Jerusalem 20:1–16
Paul addresses the
Ephesian elders   20:17–38
On to Jerusalem   21:1–14
Paul arrives in Jerusalem   21:15–26
Paul is arrested   21:27–40
Paul's defence   22:1–29
Before the Sanhedrin   22:30—23:11
Plot to kill Paul   23:12–22
Paul handed over to
Governor Felix   23:23–35
Paul before Felix   24:1–27
Before Festus   25:1–12
Before King Agrippa   25:13—26:32

Paul's journey to Rome
Paul sets sail   27:1–12
The storm and shipwreck   27:13–44
Welcome on Malta   28:1–10
Paul in Rome   28:11–31

Acts

The book of Acts covers the first 30 years of the Christian community from the ascension of Christ to Paul's house-arrest at Rome. It is the second volume of Luke's explanation of Christian beginnings. The action centres around two great Gospel advances – first, a period of home missions; second, the period of foreign missions. In the first the number of disciples jumps from 120 (1:15) to 3,120 (2:41) to 8,120 (4:4) to untold multitudes (5:14). The second advance multiplies these numbers abroad and Saul of Tarsus, once the Church's most fanatical opponent, is the leading agent of this great expansion.

Luke does not give us a *history* of the infant Church: that is, a comprehensive narrative of all the important facts. This was not his aim. Instead, under the Holy Spirit's inspiration, he concentrates on the spread of the Gospel from Jerusalem to Rome via Samaria, Antioch, Asia (in present-day Turkey) and Europe. Second century leaders gave Luke's work the title "The Acts of the Apostles", but again Luke is selective, focusing on Peter and Paul, the outstanding apostles in these areas.

The missionary Church

After Jesus ascended before the disciples to His Father, they followed His command to return to Jerusalem and wait for the Holy Spirit to be given. That happened on the Day of Pentecost. As the believers were filled and empowered by the Holy Spirit, the Church was born. Thousands of Jews from abroad listened to Peter preach the

Stephen —
Fearless and faithful

One of the first seven deacons ever to serve the Church, Stephen was an outstanding man, "full of the Holy Spirit", "full of faith" and "full of God's grace and power". In addition to his practical ministry in the distribution of food, he was a gifted preacher whose words were accompanied by wonders and miraculous signs. This quickly brought hell's opposition and Stephen became the first to follow his Lord in death.

resurrection of Jesus. 3,000 believed and were baptised.

The infant Church met constantly and increased daily. But there was sharp opposition. Excitement at a healed cripple brought arrest for Peter and John. After their setting free, a seizure of all the apostles, miraculous release and a further arrest followed.

In the Church all believers shared their possessions. Ananias and Sapphira's pretence, however, brought an awful judgment from God.

Officers were appointed to manage the distribution of food to those in need and Stephen, a powerful evangelist, was among them. Stephen's preaching brought him into conflict with the

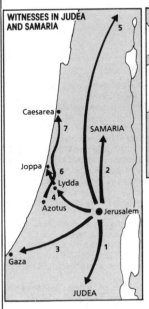

WITNESSES IN JUDEA AND SAMARIA

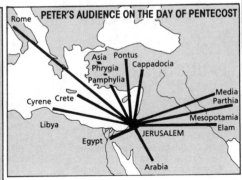

PETER'S AUDIENCE ON THE DAY OF PENTECOST

1 Persecution scatters believers throughout Judea and Samaria
2 Philip and later Peter and John preach in Samaria
3 Philip meets the Ethiopian eunuch
4 Philip continues his preaching tour
5 Paul converted to Christ during his mission to arrest Christians in Damascus
6 Peter preaches and heals in Lydda and Joppa
7 Peter brings the Gospel to Cornelius' household

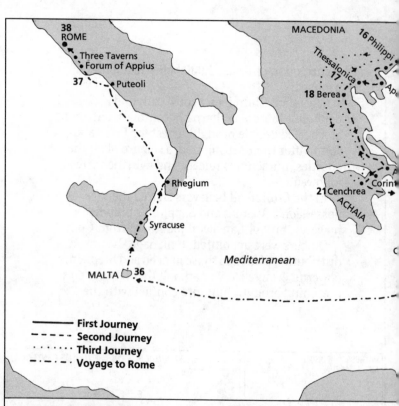

```
——————  First Journey
– – – –  Second Journey
· · · · ·  Third Journey
– · – · –  Voyage to Rome
```

PAUL'S JOURNEYS

FIRST JOURNEY

1 Saul "set apart" 13:1–3
2 Paul and companions sail to Cyprus 13:4–5
3 Paul meets sorcerer Bar-Jesus and proconsul 13:6–12
4 John Mark returns to Jerusalem 13:13
5 Paul preaches the Good News; many Gentiles believe but Jews expel Paul and Barnabas 13:14–51
6 City divided 14:1–7
7 Paul heals cripple, is called Hermes; stoned but survives 14:8–20
8 Large number of converts 14:21
9 Elders appointed 14:21–26
10 Paul reports on his first journey 14:27–28

SECOND JOURNEY

11 Paul and companions sent with letter to churches 15:22–29
12 Paul and Barnabas separate; Paul and Silas start journey 15:30–41
13 Paul chooses Timothy 16:1–5
14 The Holy Spirit keeps Paul from preaching in Asia and Bithynia 16:6–7
15 Paul's vision of a man of Macedonia; set sail for Macedonia 16:8–12
16 Conversion of Lydia; Paul casts out spirit of divination; Paul and Silas imprisoned; Philippian jailer converted; Paul and Silas freed 16:13–40
17 Paul preaches; Jews incite mob 17:1–9
18 Bereans study the message; Jews from Thessalonica stir up trouble; Paul leaves; Silas and Timothy stay 17:10–15
19 Paul preaches about the true God 17:16–34
20 Paul teaches and works; Timothy and Silas join him; Paul before Gallio 18:1–17
21 Paul sails for Syria with Priscilla and Aquila 18:18
22 Paul leaves Priscilla and Aquila 18:19–22

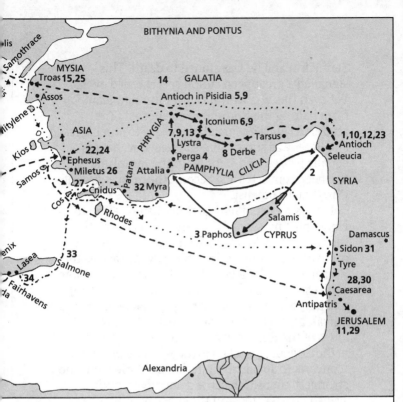

BITHYNIA AND PONTUS

MYSIA
Troas **15,25**
Assos
Samothrace
lis

ASIA
Mitylene
Kios
Ephesus **22,24**
Miletus **26**
Samos
27
Cnidus
Cos
Rhodes

GALATIA
14
Antioch in Pisidia **5,9**
PHRYGIA
Iconium **6,9**
7,9,13
Lystra
Perga **4**
Attalia
32 Myra
Patara

Tarsus
8 Derbe
PAMPHYLIA
CILICIA
1,10,12,23
Antioch
Seleucia
2
SYRIA

Salamis
3 Paphos
CYPRUS

Damascus
Sidon **31**
Tyre
28,30
Caesarea
Antipatris
JERUSALEM
11,29

enix
Lasea
Salmone
33
34
Fairhavens
da

Alexandria

THIRD JOURNEY

23 Paul strengthens the churches *18:23*
24 John's disciples receive the Holy Spirit; Paul drives out evil spirits and heals sick; seized by mob; Paul plans return to Syria; plot makes him travel through Macedonia with companions *19:1—20:6*
25 Eutychus falls from window *20:7–12*
26 Paul's farewell to the Ephesian elders *20:13–38*
27 Disciples urge Paul not to go to Jerusalem; pray with him as he sets sail *21:1–7*
28 Paul stays with Philip; Agabus' prophecy; Paul and companions go to Jerusalem *21:8–19*

FOURTH JOURNEY

29 Paul arrested; speaks to crowd; imprisoned; before Sanhedrin; plot to kill Paul *21:27—23:30*
30 Paul before Felix, Festus and Agrippa; Paul appeals to Caesar; Paul and other prisoners set sail for Italy *23:31—27:2*
31 Paul sees his friends *27:3–4*
32 Paul changes ships *27:5–6*
33 Progress slow and dangerous *27:7–8*
34 Paul warns of coming disaster *27:9–12*
35 Ship caught in storm; Paul tells sailors they will be kept safe *27:13–26*
36 Ship strikes sandbar; Paul bitten by viper; Publius' father and many others healed *27:27—28:10*
37 Paul lands in Italy; met by friends from Rome *28:11–15*
38 Paul preaches the Kingdom of God and the Lord Jesus Christ *28:16–31*

Sanhedrin and he was stoned to death. This signalled a great persecution spearheaded by Saul. Yet even this was within God's sovereign plan. Far from halting the Church, it advanced it. The scattered believers spread the Gospel to other areas and Peter was shown that the New Covenant is equally for Jew and Gentile. In the meantime Saul had been converted and become the most energetic Christian evangelist.

Peter's report of how Gentiles had received the Holy Spirit persuaded the Jerusalem church that the Gospel was for all and from this point we are captivated by a great missionary advance across the Roman world. Antioch in Syria became the mission centre for much of this activity. Here Saul (Paul) and Barnabas were set apart by the Holy Spirit and a strategic carrying of the Gospel to the urban cities of the Roman world began. Always the news of the Saviour was taken to the Jews and proselytes (converts to Judaism) first. Some believed, but the strongest opposition came generally from the Jewish quarter, too – in the shape of militant Judaizers dogging the evangelists' steps and fomenting trouble in every city.

There was a greater harvest among the Gentiles and young churches were planted in the main centres of Galatia, Asia, Macedonia and Achaia (see pages 32–33). To all the message was the same – the resurrection of Jesus and the forgiveness of sins. In all both Paul and the leaders at Jerusalem sought to express the unity there is between Jews and Gentiles in Christ.

Acts closes with Paul a prisoner at Rome, boldly preaching and teaching about the Lord who had become everything to him since that momentous turning-point on the Damascus road.

THE LETTERS

The 21 New Testament letters unfold for us many of the deep truths of the Christian faith and show the effects they should have on our daily living.

As letters written to churches, groups of churches or individuals, they are rooted in particular situations and often respond to questions raised by their readers. Thus, they give a great insight into the teaching of the apostles and the early Church, and into life and problems amongst the first Christians.

Some of the letters are the earliest New Testament writings. (1 and 2 Thessalonians, dating from c. AD 50, are probably the first.) Because their audience was well acquainted with the Gospel events, they do not record the life and teaching of Jesus. They explain, however, the significance of Christ's work – His incarnation, crucifixion, resurrection and Second Coming. In so doing, they give a picture of the Church's beliefs that is wholly in harmony with the Gospels.

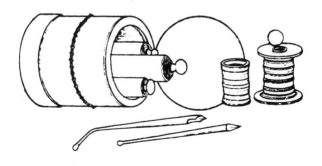

ROMANS

Paul's eagerness to visit
Rome   1:1–15
The Gospel in a nutshell   1:16–17
Paul describes the state of
the world   1:18–32

The Christian Gospel
God's righteous judgment   2:1–16
The Jews and
righteousness   2:17—3:20
Righteousness through
faith   3:21–31
The righteousness of
Abraham   4:1–25
Peace, joy and suffering   5:1–11
The Grace of God – life
through Christ   5:12–21
The old life and the new   6:1–23
A new way of serving   7:1–6
Struggling with sin   7:7–25

Living by the Spirit   8:1–17
Future glory – more than
conquerors   8:18–39

Grief for Israel
God's sovereign choice   9:1–33
Confessing Jesus   10:1–21
The remnant of Israel   11:1–10
Natural and wild branches   11:11–32
Song of praise   11:33–36

The Christian life
Sacrificial living and love   12:1–21
Submission to authorities   13:1–7
Love, for the day is near   13:8–14
Helping a weak brother   14:1–23
Christ's example   15:1–13
Paul's plans and final
greetings   15:14—16:27

Romans

Paul probably wrote this letter from Corinth in about AD 57 on his third missionary journey. The task of taking the relief fund to Jerusalem lay before him, but he hoped to visit Rome some day. Little did he know the sequence of events by which God would soon bring him to that city.

In Rome, the diplomatic and trade heart of the Empire, a strong Christian community of Jews and Gentiles was flourishing already. To them Paul gives his fullest explanation of the Gospel. His theme – faith in Christ as the only grounds of acceptance by God and the freedom, with our sins cleansed, to live by the Spirit as the sons of God. The letter is a summary of the key truths that Paul taught in the churches where he spent some time proclaiming the Gospel.

Righteousness from God

In the opening chapter of his letter to the Roman Christians Paul rejoices in their faith and opens his heart to them – speaking of his eagerness to visit and minister to them. The force that impels him is the dynamic of the Gospel – "the power of God for the salvation of everyone who believes" (v. 16). Having presented this "Gospel in a nutshell", he goes on to outline the depths of human sin and God's righteous anger against mankind.

Paul explains the key truth in how we come to know God – on the basis of faith in Jesus Christ who died for us while we were still sinners (5:8).

The apostle begins by demonstrating that all – both the Jews who knew the Law and the Gentiles who did not – are under the power of sin and are powerless to keep the Law themselves. The glory of the Good News is that God gives us a righteousness Himself through faith in Christ. Abraham was accepted by God on these grounds, Paul shows.

So some ask: "Can we go on sinning?" By no means! The apostle sweeps this suggestion away showing that the Christian has died to his old life and is no longer a slave to sin, but a slave to righteousness.

Paul discusses the position of Israel in God's purposes and explains that in Israel, as among the Gentiles, God chooses to save whom He wills. Still he stresses his heart's prayer for Israel and belief that God yet has a special plan for her.

From chapter 12 the letter takes a practical turn as Paul urges the church to respond to God's love and live a life of surrender to God and love and acceptance of one another.

ROMANS: THE GOSPEL EXPLAINED

It is:	It brings:

The Gospel of God *(1:1)*
  – promised in the Scriptures *(1:2)*
  – regarding God's Son *(1:3)*
  – of God's Son *(1:9)*
  – the power of God *(1:16)*
  – revealing God's wrath against sin *(1:18)*
  – revealing righteousness from God by faith *(1:17)*
	Righteousness from God *(3:21)*
	  – through faith in Christ *(3:22)*
	Free justification *(3:24)*
	  – by Christ's atoning death *(3:25)*
	Peace with God *(5:1)*
	God's love poured into our hearts *(5:5)*
	The gift of the Holy Spirit *(5:5)*
	Rescue from God's wrath *(5:9)*
	Eternal life through Christ *(5:21)*
	Death to the old sinful life *(6:2)*
	Resurrection to the new life *(6:4)*
	Slavery to righteousness *(6:18)*
	Life by the Spirit *(8:9)*
	Victory in all hardship *(8:37)*

Christ in glory. 15th C. Cyprus.

1 CORINTHIANS

The divisions in the church

Greetings and exhortations to unity	1:1–17
Foolishness and wisdom	1:18—2:5
God's secret wisdom	2:6–16
On divisions in the church	3:1–22
Pride and arrogance	4:1–21

The disorders in the church

Sexual immorality	5:1–13
Lawsuits amongst believers	6:1–11
Sins against the body	6:12–20

The difficulties in the church

Questions about marriage	7:1–40
Food offered to idols	8:1–13
Forgoing rights	9:1–27
A warning from history	10:1–13
Idol feasts and the Lord's Supper	10:14–22
Matters of conscience	10:23–33
Propriety in worship	11:1–16
Disorder and the Lord's Supper	11:17–34
Spiritual gifts	12:1–31
The best gift is love	13:1–13
Gifts of prophecy and tongues	14:1–39
The resurrection	15:1–58
Final instructions and greetings	16:1–24

2 CORINTHIANS

Paul's ministry

The God of all comfort	1:1–11
Paul's change of plans	1:12—2:4
The aroma of Christ	2:5—3:6
The glory of the New Covenant	3:7–18
Treasure in jars of clay	4:1–18
The earthly tent	5:1–10
Message of reconciliation	5:11—6:2
Paul's hardships	6:3–13
A clean break	6:14—7:1
Paul's joy	7:2–16

The collection

Generous giving	8:1—9:5
Sowing and reaping	9:6–15

Paul's credentials

Paul answers his critics	10:1—11:15
Paul's sufferings	11:16–33
Paul's vision and his thorn	12:1–10
Paul's concern for the Corinthians	12:11–21
The coming visit	13:1–10
Final greetings	13:11–14

1 Corinthians

Corinth was a bustling commercial city. Its
cosmopolitan make-up was reflected in the
church. Unhappily, there were many tensions and
faults within it.

While Paul was at Ephesus during his third
missionary journey, news from Chloe's household
in Corinth reached him of immorality and
divisions within the church. Three members of the
church also came to obtain advice on pressing
issues: marriage, food sacrificed to idols, spiritual
gifts and charitable collections. In about AD 54
Paul wrote his first letter to the Corinthians to deal
with all these matters.

On to maturity

Paul's letter is launched with an appeal for unity in
Christ. Groups had developed claiming to be of
Paul, of Apollos, of Cephas (Peter) and (as if no one
else belonged to Him) of Christ. To these the
apostle says Paul, Apollos and Cephas are nothing –
only servants of Christ. Mindful of the creeping
influences of Greek philosophy and mystical
religions, he reminds them, too, that they owe
nothing to any man-made wisdom. Their
redemption and knowledge of God came only
because they are in Christ.

Paul is saddened at the church's immaturity and
shocked that gross immorality has been allowed to
continue among some of its members. Such
should be put out of the fellowship, he says. He
gives instructions on marriage to Christian
couples, to partners married to non-Christians and
advice to singles.

Answering the problem of food at the market-place which had been offered in pagan sacrifices, Paul stresses both the Christian's freedom to eat and his responsibility to weaker believers who may only recently have been delivered from pagan worship. To support this advice, he speaks of his own surrender of an apostle's rights for the sake of the Gospel. The guiding principle is this – whatever we do, we should be careful not to cause others to stumble, but do everything to the glory of God. Paul continues his practical instructions, first concerning the woman's covering of the head in public worship and then behaviour at the Lord's Supper.

Turning his attention to spiritual gifts, he addresses the Corinthians' awe for the spectacular gifts and the feelings of inferiority felt by those who lacked them. Paul points out that all spiritual gifts are sovereignly given by the Holy Spirit. They are for the benefit of the whole church. No-one is superior or inferior and all should have equal love and concern for each other. Indeed, the apostle shows that the greatest gift is love. Without it the others are useless.

Some in the church were falling into serious error and denying the resurrection of the body. This is to deny Christ's resurrection, too, Paul says, as he reminds them of the central fact of Jesus' triumph over death. Paul goes on to answer their questions about the mystery of our resurrection bodies.

Paul –
Apostle with unlimited horizons

With his sights set fixedly on the extermination of Christianity, Saul could never have imagined the transformation God was to accomplish in his life. Yet he later recognised (Gal. 1:15–16) that even from birth God was preparing him for his ministry as an apostle.

Although a proud Jew, from his childhood in the Graeco-Roman city of Tarsus he had known the Gentile world. With his Roman citizenship (Acts 22:28) he had a passport to travel and a diplomatic immunity before unjust magistrates. Trained under leading Rabbi Gamaliel (Acts 22:3), he had developed the intellectual abilities that made him the foremost explainer of Christian theology and an able spokesman before kings and governors. His zealous and practical nature and burning compassion for lost men and women made him no armchair theologian.

Paul's conversion turned his remarkable gifts and privileges to God's service. From being a leader of orthodox Judaism (Gal. 1:14) he immediately became an urgent preacher of the Gospel (Acts 9:20).

Through his missions Paul planted churches in many of the strategic centres of the Mediterranean world. He chose and trained men to lead those churches on to maturity. He claimed no rights for himself, but was above all a servant of the Gospel and those to whom God sent him.

Paul did not have an impressive appearance or produce dazzling oratory (2 Cor. 10:10). He frequently suffered for the Gospel. He knew physical weakness. Yet his influence for Christ is probably unequalled. The secret is that he was totally dependent on the empowering and resources of Christ (2 Cor. 12:9).

2 Corinthians

This letter gives a unique understanding of the burdens of Paul's apostleship and its cost to him in personal terms. His last letter to the Corinthian church had been written with many tears and an unscheduled visit following it had been very painful. It is now about a year later and he has hastened to Macedonia to receive news of them from Titus.

The apostle describes the glory of the ministry God has given him and his co-worker, Timothy, and God's power that enables them to overcome the pressures they face. The catalogue of their sufferings commends them as servants of God.

Paul is overjoyed at Titus' news that his last letter has produced repentance in the church. Now he mentions to them the relief fund for the poor in Jerusalem and encourages them to give liberally. Finally, he turns his attention to a minority who still view him as a second-rate apostle. Paul defends his authority, reminds them of his sacrifices for the Gospel and asks them to examine themselves and put things right before he comes to them.

GALATIANS

The Gospel defended and explained

No other Gospel	1:1–10
Paul's experience – called by God	1:11–24
Accepted by the apostles	2:1–10
Paul opposes Peter	2:11–21
Prisoners under the law	3:1–25
Sons of God	3:26—4:7
Paul's concern for the Galatians	4:8–31

The Gospel applied

Freedom in Christ	5:1–15
Life by the Spirit	5:16—6:18

EPHESIANS

The believer's position in Christ

God's eternal purpose	1:1–14
Paul's prayer	1:15–23
One in Christ	2:1–22
Paul's mission to the Gentiles	3:1–13
Paul's prayer for the Ephesians	3:14–21

The believer's walk in the world

Christian unity	4:1–16
Children of light	4:17—5:21
Christian relationships	5:22—6:9
The armour of God	6:10–24

LETTERS TO CHURCHES

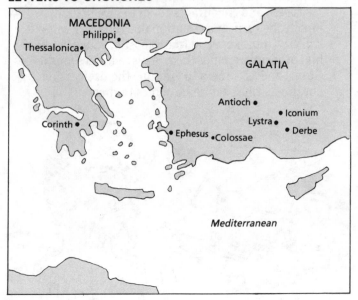

Galatians

After Paul had founded the churches in Galatia (in present-day Turkey), other Jewish teachers had arrived insisting that the Gentile converts should be circumcised and observe the Jewish law.

Paul was distraught. In his most strongly-worded epistle, he condemns these Jewish teachers and demonstrates that there is no Gospel given by God other than that he has preached – it is not by keeping the Law that anyone is saved, but by faith in Christ. Whether Jew or Gentile, the Galatian Christians are all God's children by virtue of Christ dwelling in them by His Spirit. Freed from the impossible burden of keeping the Law by their own efforts, they are to live by the Spirit who will reproduce Christ in them.

Ephesians

The date was the early 60's. Paul was writing while under house arrest in Rome what was probably a circular letter to the churches in Ephesus and the surrounding region in Western Turkey.

Although in confinement, Paul's spirit was not chained. Ephesians is full of praise. In the first chapter Paul considers the Father's choice of His people before creation, the fulness of believers' blessings in Christ and the seal of the Holy Spirit guaranteeing their place in heaven.

From this he prays that his readers should understand the fulness of God's power and know that the Son is Lord over all and is reigning on behalf of the church.

In his second chapter the apostle reminds the Ephesians of the revolution God's grace has brought in their lives. Gentiles without God have been brought into His family – Jew and Gentile are made one through the cross.

Paul prays that his readers may know the full dimensions of Christ's love and urges them to live worthy of their position in Christ. Instructions for church, individual, family and work life show what he means.

DATING THE NEW TESTAMENT

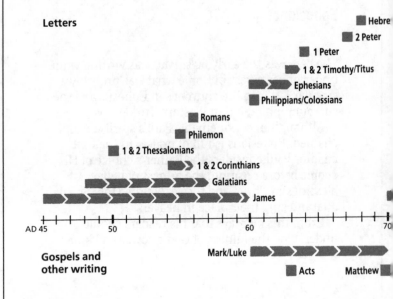

PHILIPPIANS

Paul's heart outpoured

Thanksgiving and prayer	1:1–11
In chains for Christ	1:12–30
The attitude of Christ	2:1–18
Timothy and Epaphroditus	2:19–30
The true circumcision	3:1–11
Towards the goal	3:12–21
Encouragement and thanks	4:1–23

COLOSSIANS

The Lordship of Christ

Paul's prayer	1:1–14
Christ's supremacy	1:15–23
Paul's task	1:24—2:5
Wrong teaching and right attitudes	2:6—3:4
Take off the old self, put on the new	3:5—4:6
Personal news	4:7–18

1 THESSALONIANS

Personal reflections

Thanksgiving for their faith	1:1–10
Paul recalls his visit	2:1–20
Encouraging report	3:1–13

Anticipating the Lord's return

Living to please God	4:1–12
Our Lord's return	4:13—5:11
Final exhortations	5:12–28

2 THESSALONIANS

The Second Coming of Christ

Encouragement	1:1–12
Events leading up to Christ's return	2:1–12
Stand firm	2:13—3:5
Against idleness	3:6–18

This chart shows the approximate date of writing of each New Testament book.
Where there is uncertainty over the precise period of writing, longer, arrowed lines appear.

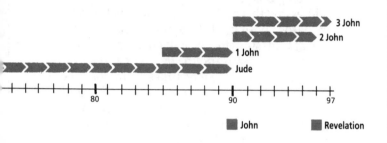

3 John

2 John

1 John

Jude

80   90   97

■ John   ■ Revelation

Philippians

Again Paul writes from prison, but the situation appears more serious than in Ephesians and death is a real possibility (1:20–22). Yet, Paul's letter to the church in the Roman colony of Philippi is one of the most joyful and beautiful epistles.

The apostle has a warm affection for the Philippians. He rejoices in their partnership in the Gospel and encourages them to see that his chains are advancing, not hindering, God's purposes. The apostle exhorts the Philippians to imitate Christ who, though God, humbled Himself to death on the cross. He urges them to press on in the Christian life, as Paul does himself, and closes thanking them for their gifts to him.

Colossians

Paul had never visited the Colossian church, but had heard of their progress from Epaphras, a leader there. It caused Paul to rejoice in their faith, but he was concerned that human philosophies were also influencing them.

Addressing this problem, Paul says that they have all they need in Christ alone. Christ is the image of God, supreme over all creation. He has conquered sin, death and the devil and brought reconciliation to God. So he urges them not to be misled by empty Greek philosophy (2:8), by those stressing the Jewish Law (2:16) or by asceticism (denying the body because only the soul was thought to be good – 2:23). Instead, they are to grow up into Christ and live as God's holy people.

1 and 2 Thessalonians

These were two of Paul's first letters sent (about AD 50) to the second congregation Paul and his friends founded in Europe.

Paul was overjoyed at Timothy's good news of the Thessalonians' progress in spite of persecution. Directions are given to live holy lives, to win the respect of outsiders by being good workers and particular teaching is given about the Lord's Second Coming.

The second letter, written shortly afterwards, gives a further explanation about the end times, for it seems Paul's first letter had been misunderstood and they were thinking the Day of the Lord was at hand.

Idleness was a problem at Thessalonica which anticipation of Christ's coming had increased. Paul warns against it – there was no such behaviour from the apostle and his co-workers.

ON ACTIVE SERVICE

Seated with Christ in the heavenly realms. Jesus the crucified, risen, ascended and glorified Lord has won this place for His people (Eph. 2:4–7). Christ triumphed over Satan (Col. 2:15) on the cross and the enemy's final destruction is certain (Rev. 20:10). Now, however, Christ entrusts the battle to His Church. Every Christian is to train in both offensive and defensive warfare. There is no reason to feel inadequate for the power at our disposal is Christ's: "Be strong in the Lord and in his mighty power" (Eph. 6:10).

Paul pictures the Christian as a soldier (Eph. 6:10–17; 2 Tim. 2:3–4). He has been given many pieces of armour and is to make use of them all. As he does, he is to grasp the weapon of prayer and pray in the Spirit on all occasions. With God's power and protection used, he will know victory and see territory taken for Christ.

ASPECTS OF PRAYER

The Lord's prayer	Mt. 6:9–15; Lk. 11:1–4
Jesus' public prayers	Mt. 11:25–26; Jn. 11:41–42; Jn. 17
Jesus' high priestly prayer	Jn. 17
The Church together	Acts 1:14, 4:24–31, 12:5, 13, 21:5
Singly in private	Mt. 6:5–6; Mk. 1:35, 6:46; Lk. 5:16, 6:12
Answers promised	Mt. 7:7–11; Lk. 11:9–13; Jn. 15:7, 16:23–24; 1 Jn. 5:14–15

Conditions for successful prayer

Forgiving others	Mt. 6:14–15; Mk. 11:25
Humility	Lk. 18:9–14
In faith	Mk. 11:22–24; James 4:3
In God's will	Mt. 26:39, 42; Mk. 14:35–36; Lk. 22:42; 2 Cor. 12:7–9; 1 Jn. 5:14
Obedience	1 Jn. 3:21–22
Righteousness	James 5:16
Right motives	James 4:3

The Holy Spirit's help	Rom. 8:26–27
Our needs known by God	Mt. 6:7–8
Continuance in prayer	Lk. 18:1–8; Eph. 6:18; 1 Thess. 5:17
Earnestness	Lk. 22:44; Acts 12:5; James 5:17
Boldness	Lk. 11:5–8
Agreement in prayer	Mt. 18:19
In temptation	Mt. 26:41; Mk. 14:38; Lk. 22:40–46
For Christian maturity	Eph. 1:15–23, 3:14–21; Phil. 1:9–11
For proclamation of the Gospel	Eph. 6:19–20
For those in authority	1 Tim. 2:1–2
Praise and thanksgiving	Mt. 11:25–26; Lk. 1:46–55, 2:20, 19:37–38; Phil. 4:6; Col. 1:12, 3:15; 1 Thess. 5:18; Rev. 7:10–12, 11:15–18, 19:5
As incense before God	Rev. 5:8, 8:3

Christ at prayer from an Italian mosaic.

1 TIMOTHY

Directions to a young pastor

False teachings	1:1–11
God's grace to Paul	1:12–20
Holiness and worship	2:1–15
Church leaders	3:1–16
Teach the truth	4:1–16
On widows, elders and slaves	5:1—6:2
Love of money and real wealth	6:3–21

2 TIMOTHY

Be faithful in pastoring

Be faithful	1:1—2:13
Hold to the truth	2:14–26
Godlessness in the last days	3:1–9
Paul's charge and final requests	3:10–22

TITUS

The conduct of the church

Titus' task on Crete	1:1–16
Christian conduct	2:1—3:2
Stressing the Gospel	3:3–11
Final instructions	3:12–15

PHILEMON

Paul's gratitude	1–7
Paul's plea	8–25

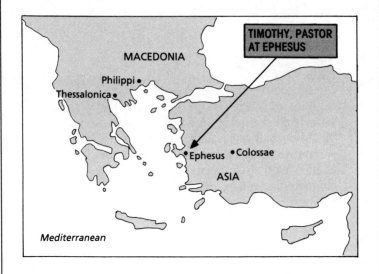

1 and 2 Timothy

Together with Titus, these letters are commonly
known as the "pastoral epistles". To young pastors
Paul gives advice on fulfilling their responsibilities.
To Timothy he gives directions on qualifications
for overseers (elders) and deacons. He stresses
Bible-centred teaching which will promote
Christian truth and godliness, gives guidance on
practical care in the fellowship and personal
exhortations to Timothy himself.

While 1 Timothy was written during a period of
freedom after Paul's first imprisonment, the
second letter comes from a final Roman
confinement as he was awaiting execution. The
letter contains the apostle's last recorded words.
Paul encourages Timothy to be faithful to his
calling and facing death himself, he urges: "Endure
hardship – preach the Word".

Titus

Titus had been left behind in Crete to consolidate
Paul's work. It was not an easy task! Titus'
responsibility was to teach the rather undisciplined
Cretans with all authority so that the believers'
characters would be an advertisement for the
Saviour.

Philemon

This is a personal letter to Philemon, a Christian in Colossae, and a plea for one of his slaves. The slave, Onesimus, had stolen some money and run away, but in Rome he had come into contact with Paul and been converted.

Paul sent Onesimus back, but with this letter, confidently asking Philemon to be lenient and welcome him as a brother in the Lord.

THE NEW TESTAMENT CANON

During the times of the apostles, the New Testament writings were being circulated and read among the churches and were given the same respect as the Old Testament Scriptures. As the Church entered the second century, a process of collecting the books together began. This also meant distinguishing those which were divinely inspired from false writings which appeared.

In fact the Church never had any real difficulty in recognising the false writings. The only possibility by the middle of the second century was of omitting some books like James and Jude which were not by the apostles. Unanimous recognition of the New Testament as we have it today came at the end of the fourth century. It is important to remember, however, that our acceptance of the New Testament documents does not rest on their inclusion in the Church's canonical lists. Rather, the Church listed them because God's people had always recognised them as the authentic words of God to men.

HEBREWS

The pre-eminence of Christ

The Son – superior to
angels — 1:1—2:4

Jesus Christ, the Son of
Man — 2:5–18

Jesus – greater than Moses — 3:1–19

A sabbath-rest for the
people of God — 4:1–13

Our great High Priest — 4:14—5:10

Warning and
encouragement — 5:11—6:20

Melchizedek the priest — 7:1–10

Jesus Christ – high priest
of a new covenant — 7:11—8:13

Worship in the earthly
tabernacle — 9:1–10

The blood of Christ — 9:11–28

The perfect sacrifice — 10:1–18

The life of faith

A call to persevere — 10:19–39

By faith — 11:1–40

The Father's discipline — 12:1–13

Warning against resisting
God — 12:14–29

Living to please God — 13:1–25

Timothy – Making of a minister

"I have no-one else like him ... because as a son with his father he has served with me in the work of the gospel" (Phil. 2:20, 22). Paul's words about Timothy reveal the deep affection and respect he had for his young co-labourer.

Timothy had been converted through Paul's preaching and, in spite of his natural reserve and frequent ailments, he was a willing companion on Paul's dangerous travels, a trusted representative and a faithful pastor to the churches he was sent to.

Hebrews

If the Gospel brings persecution and Judaism did not, why not return to Judaism? The letter to the Hebrews was written to Jewish Christians facing this temptation.

It shows that the Old Covenant – now obsolete – was just a shadow of the New. Christ is the climax of God's revelation – His exact representation. The Old Testament priesthood and sacrifices were copies of the real things. Jesus, the great High Priest, has made the real sacrifice for our sins and entered heaven itself on our behalf.

With the example of the Old Testament men of faith behind them, the readers are encouraged to persevere through opposition in the light of the glorious salvation they have in Christ.

JAMES

Faith in action

Trials and temptations	1:1–18
Listening and doing	1:19–27
No discrimination	2:1–13
Faith and actions	2:14–26
Taming the tongue	3:1–12
Wisdom and submission to God	3:13—4:17
Rich oppressors	5:1–6
Patience and believing prayer	5:7–20

1 PETER

The living hope

Our hope in Christ	1:1–12
Call to holy living	1:13—2:12
Submission to rulers	2:13–25
Husbands and wives	3:1–7
Prepared to suffer	3:8—4:19
To elders and young men	5:1–14

2 PETER

Exhortation and warning

Knowing God and His message	1:1–21
False teachers and their destruction	2:1–22
The Day of the Lord	3:1–18

THE CHURCHES PETER WROTE TO

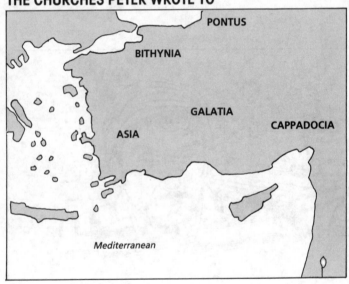

James

Action, not just words. This is what James' letter is about. He calls believers to active Christian living, allowing their faith to affect every part of their lives and conduct. James does not deny that we are saved by faith (2:5), but stresses that true faith is shown in action (2:18).

The letter is probably one of the earliest New Testament writings (AD 45?) and its most likely author is James, the Lord's brother, who became a leader in the church at Jerusalem.

1 and 2 Peter

"Feed my sheep." Peter did not forget these words of Jesus to him before the Lord's ascension. In his letters Peter's pastoral concern is very clear. Both were probably sent to groups in the five Roman provinces mentioned in the opening words of the first letter. It is likely that he wrote the first from Rome at the outbreak of Nero's persecutions of the Church (AD 64).

The message of 1 Peter is to think on the Christian's glorious hope and privileges and to live pure lives before God. Suffering is coming to Peter's readers as it is to Peter himself, so he exhorts them to stand firm.

2 Peter followed a few years later (AD 67?). The apostle stresses the inspiration of the Scriptures upon which believers must take their stand. False prophets would come along teaching heresy and behaving shamefully. Scoffers would appear saying, "Where is this 'coming' Jesus promised?" Christians must not be deceived by either group, but grow in the grace and knowledge of Christ.

James –
Brother of the Lord

Although the brother of Jesus, James, like the Lord's other brothers, does not seem to have accepted Jesus' Messiahship until the resurrection. It was this which turned him into a convinced believer. We are told in 1 Corinthians 15:7 of Christ's personal post-resurrection appearance to James and we know Jesus' brothers gathered with the disciples in the upper room at Pentecost. After Pentecost, as leader of the Jerusalem church, James was visited by Saul following his conversion and James presided over the "Jerusalem council" which ruled that Gentile Christians did not need circumcision or to keep the laws of Moses.

1 JOHN

God is life and light
The Word of Life 1:1–4
Children of the light 1:5—2:17
Warning against antichrists 2:18–27

Children of God
The children of God 2:28—3:24
Test the spirits 4:1–6
This is love 4:7–21
Assurance of eternal life 5:1–21

2 JOHN

Live in love and obedience 1–13

3 JOHN

Encouragement to Gaius 1–13

JUDE

The condemnation of
godless men 1–16
A call to persevere 17–25

1 John

1 John is full of teaching and comfort for Christians of every age. Yet knowing about the particular situation facing John's original readers will help us understand some of the letter's more difficult parts.

The apostle wrote to Christians shaken by false teaching. Some who had professed to be believers were following Greek philosophical views that the soul was good and the flesh evil. They denied Christ's divinity, claiming that God was too pure to become flesh, and justified sinful behaviour on the basis that only the soul was good so the body could do whatever it pleased.

Thus, John declares loud and clear the message of which he was an eye-witness – Jesus is God the Son, come in the flesh. Anyone who denies it does not belong to Him. Those who are His have the Holy Spirit – they know the truth and they do not continue in lives of sin.

2 and 3 John

2 and 3 John show the same background as John's first letter. John encourages the believers to continue in the truth and in love for one another. He exhorts them to reject teachers who reject the Gospel and to welcome those who proclaim it.

Jude

Jude, the younger brother of the Lord and James, had been so alarmed by news of false teachers among his readers that he wrote a quite different letter to the one he had intended. He urges the faithful Christians to contend for the faith, to build themselves up in it and to do all they can to rescue others from the deadly influences of false teaching and from eternal judgment.

JESUS WORSHIPPED...

Saints singing to the Lamb 14th cent.

At His birth	*Matt. 2:2, 11*
After walking on the water	*Matt. 14:33*
By a man born blind	*John 9:38*
After the Resurrection	*Matt. 28:9, 17*
At the Ascension	*Luke 24:52*
By the angels	*Hebrews 1:6*
In Heaven	*Rev. 5:8, 12–14*

That all worship is to be directed to the Lord God (Yahweh) is the clear teaching of the first two Commandments (*Ex. 20:3–6*) and of Jesus (*Mt. 4:10*). Yet the Son of God received and accepted such worship – a clear declaration of His divinity.

REVELATION

Messages to the seven churches
Introduction: John's vision
of Christ | 1:1–20
To the seven churches | 2:1–3:22

Opening the book with seven seals
John's vision of heaven | 4:1–11
The scroll and the Lamb | 5:1–14
The seven seals | 6:1–8:5
The trumpets | 8:6–9:21

The hour of reckoning
The little scroll and the two
witnesses | 10:1–11:14
The seventh trumpet | 11:15–19
The woman and the dragon | 12:1–17
The two beasts | 13:1–18
The joy of the redeemed
and the harvest | 14:1–20

God pours out His wrath
The seven last plagues | 15:1–16:21

The defeat of evil
The woman on the beast | 17:1–18
The fall of Babylon | 18:1–24
Hallelujah! The
wedding-feast of the Lamb | 19:1–10
Christ victorious | 19:11–21
The thousand years | 20:1–6
The overthrow of Satan | 20:7–10
The Last Judgment | 20:11–15

God's new creation
The new Jerusalem | 21:1–27
The river of life | 22:1–6
Christ is coming soon | 22:7–17
Final warning | 22:18–19
Come, Lord Jesus | 22:20–21

Ephesus – Leading city of the Roman province of Asia.

Smyrna – A main city and port on Asia's west coast. Polycarp was Smyrna's bishop, martyred AD 155.

Pergamum – A strongly pagan city. The site of the first temple for emperor worship, of a great altar to Zeus ("Satan's seat"?) and a centre for the cult of Asklepios.

Thyatira – Commercial centre on the road East. It played no significant part in later Church history.

Sardis – Former capital of the ancient kingdom of Lydia.

Philadephia – A small town in a fertile farming area. A Christian witness was maintained here into modern times.

Laodicea – A rich commercial city, able to fund its rebuilding programme without the Senate's relief aid following a disastrous earthquake. Banking, the sale of wool and eye-salve were sources of income.

Revelation

The theme of Revelation is the victory of Christ and
His Church over Satan and his helpers. No matter
how things may look, God is King over all, Christ is
coming again to destroy Satan and his servants,
and to establish a new heaven and a new earth
where God will be with His people for ever. The
book's title, Revelation (*Apocalypse* in Greek)
simply means "unveiling" as it draws back the
curtain to show the reality behind the earthly
scene.

Revelation contains much that is difficult to
understand – it is not surprising that many
Christians have had different views of how best to
interpret it. It is worth noting that Revelation is a
book of visions, employing many symbols and
images which need not be understood too literally.
It will be helpful, too, to see that there is a cyclic
pattern to the visions – they return repeatedly to

THE SEVEN LETTERS OF REVELATION

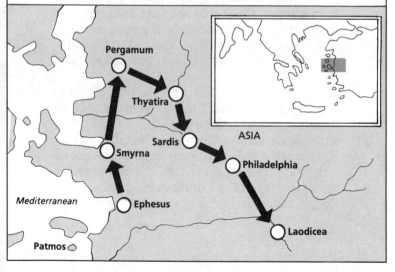

the same events and view them from different perspectives.

A certain hope

The apostle John was an exile for his faith on Patmos when Jesus appeared to him. Probably he had been sentenced to hard labour in the island's quarries under the persecution of the Emperor Domitian (AD 81–96). In this period of opposition Christ came to His servant and revealed "what is now and what will take place later" (1:19).

First John is given seven letters to the churches of his own day in Asia Minor. The exhortations and encouragements to live in the light of Christ's rewards to the faithful are relevant to Christians of every age. Following the letters there is a shift of perspective – to a vision of heaven showing God reigning over all.

The seven seals reveal God's judgments upon the earth and His protection for His people. Six trumpets again herald judgments upon mankind and the seventh trumpet announces the end: Jesus reigns; the time for judging the dead has come. John is shown the present troubles and future glory of the redeemed, then he is given a vision of seven bowls of God's wrath outpoured on the earth and "Babylon" – a mighty power opposed to God – falls.

Christ now receives His bride, the Church; Satan and his helpers are cast into the lake of fire and the resurrection and judgment of all men takes place. A new heaven and earth are revealed and God's Spirit and the bride invite our response: "Whoever is thirsty, let him come" and "take ... the free gift of the water of life". The Lord is coming soon – the Church responds: "Amen. Come, Lord Jesus."